She Took a Deep Breath In Time

Suzanne Overholt Stelling

This is Book Two in a series entitled *She Took A Deep Breath*.

Thank you, sweet Handsome, for your encouragement.
Thank you, Bryan and Jody, for your publishing guidance.
Thank You, dear Trinity, for drawing me closer through … *In Time*.

© Suzanne Overholt Stelling, 2016
All photography and text by Suzanne Stelling
suzannestelling@mac.com to book retreats

ISBN: 978-1-970037-22-7

Also available on Amazon.com, Barnesandnoble.com, and in a variety of retail locations: *She Took A Deep Breath*.
For bulk orders and group discount information, contact the publisher at dyer.cbpublishing@gmail.com.

Scriptures taken from the Holy Bible, New International Version®, NIV®. Copyright © 1973, 1978, 1984, 2011 by Biblica, Inc.™ Used by permission of Zondervan. All rights reserved worldwide. www.zondervan.com. The "NIV" and "New International Version" are trademarks registered in the United States Patent and Trademark Office by Biblica, Inc.™

Glaciers tell a good story.

I find they are similar to people:
they've been built up, and they've melted;
they've been pure blue ice, and they've been messy with dirt;
they've looked impenetrable, but are actively falling into pieces.
Just look at the cover and consider what you see.

Glaciers remodel landscapes through slow movement and weight. I think God does the same with our souls.
Using the weight of His own glory and grace, He reshapes us over time. One of the ways He is actively doing that
within me is the ancient practice of the seven sacred pauses (7SP),
a spiritual discipline that intentionally refocuses attention and energy Godward.
Since I have been transformed by it slowly, over years, I thought you might enjoy this Biblical practice too.

For the fifth pause, I recommend the Examen, and have written it into that time slot.
A summary of the 7SP and the Examen are in the back of this book, as well as a photo index.

There are several helpful websites for more information about the 7SP and the Examen.
My two favorites are theexameneffort.com and www.ignatianspirituality.com.

Enjoy! May this visual call to worship and attention enrich your intimacy with the Trinity.
Much love in Jesus,
Suzanne Stelling

The Morning

She took a deep breath and waited for God in the morning.

THE QUIET of the morning feels holy,
like being on tiptoe with great anticipation of something or SomeOne beautiful.
I wait for You like that, Father — on tiptoe. Come to me, Father. I know You will.

THE MORNING

She took a deep breath and arose for the day.

Oh Lord, as the sun rises, so I arise and delight in You.
As the day rises from the night, so do I experience a little resurrection.
I count on Your grace to sustain me and Your truth to guide me.
I walk by faith, not by sight.

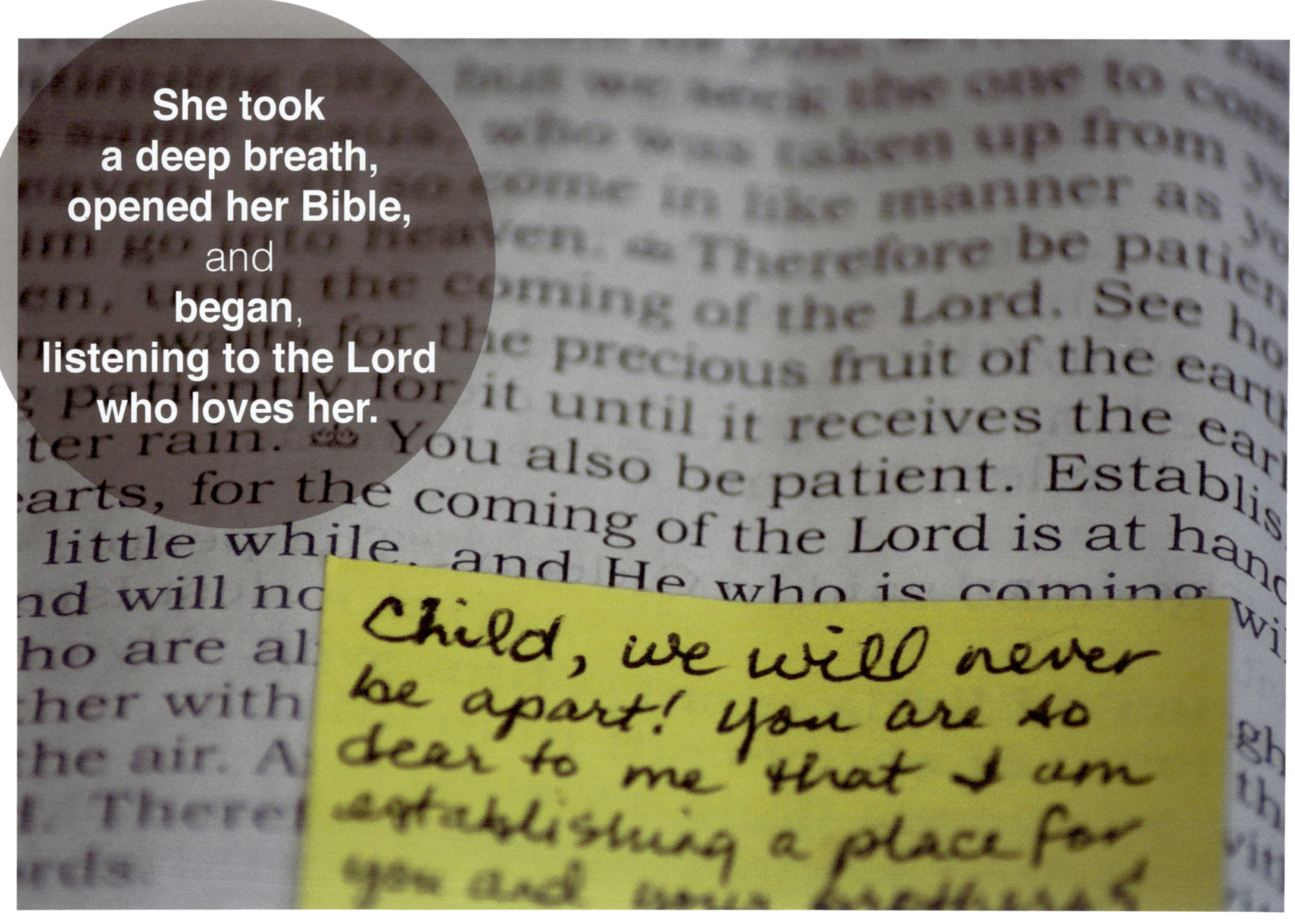

She took a deep breath, opened her Bible, and began, listening to the Lord who loves her.

OH GOD, Your words bring LIFE. How vital it is that I make time for You.
How dearly I love Your voice in my soul!
Speak, Lord. Your servant is listening.

THE MORNING

She took a deep breath and enjoyed the peace and quiet.

YOU ARE A MIST-MAKER, stealthily bringing life-giving water, keeping stillness and quiet in the land, giving the place one more slow breath before the bright sun calls everything into activity. Please, Lord, bring it to my heart as well.

She took a deep breath and treasured the morning.

IT'S WORTH GETTING UP EARLY to see You work in the quiet of a new day.
I like catching You creating beauty — beauty that is often unseen, unnoticed, unapplauded.
Just look at Your sunbeams breaking through the pines!
Break through anything within me that hinders Your light.

She took a deep breath and watched in wonder.

HIDDEN MARVEL, this industrious swallow, navigating through fog, finding flotsam floating.
Your creation stirs, hungry.
We look to You for physical and spiritual food this morning.
Good Father, give us this day our daily bread.

She took a deep breath and began brightly.

I AM FILLED WITH JOY, knowing I am Yours and You are mine.
I live as a child of light even in the gray hues of where I move and work.
May Your face shine on me, and may Your blessings fall on me,
that the world may be covered in signs of Your love.

Mid-Morning: the Value of Work

She took a deep breath and stopped trying to blend in.

TO BE YOURS, to be used of You this day,
I commit fearlessly to being Your unique child commissioned by You to do my unique work.
Your Kingdom come, Your will be done, on earth as it is in heaven.

She took a deep breath and committed her day to God's glory.

EVEN ORDINARY DAYS in ordinary lives can seem extraordinary to an onlooker. Whether I fish or sew or cook or run a city, whether I invest in little people or the stock exchange, Lord, may I worship you as I work today.

> She took a deep breath and looked for God.

Abba, Father, are You here?
Are You in the midst of my days, my grocery shopping, my tending to life, my everyday duties?
Do You see me here in the middle of *normal*, of simple and plain and ordinary?

Because I am made in Your image, Lord, I am creative.
Help me to create things of beauty and usefulness. May I be a contributor to Your kingdom.
Weave Your colors into the fabric of our lives.

She took a deep breath and **worked through one detail at a time.**

I'VE GOT A LOT TO DO.

In You my work, the stuff of earth — vocation, relationship, and community — is sacred.

I work courageously and lovingly with all my heart for You.

Please be with me as all of my small tasks add up to my one life.

She took a deep breath and acknowledged the world in front of her.

FATHER, from farmland and field, from commuters and computers, from high-rise and hometown, tell me: what is my goal, wherever and however I work?

To love You with all my heart, soul, mind, and strength, and to love my neighbor as myself.

She took a deep breath and embraced wisdom.

As I AM immersed in this workday, help me abide in You
and apply Your wisdom
in my transactions, relationships, and dealings.
I want my interactions to trigger love and prayer.

She took a deep breath and basked in God's love.

YOU WORKED six days, creating with Wisdom at Your side, full of joy.
How brilliant You are! How remarkable, how stunning are Your works!
I love to see how You have created electrons to elephants, pistils to people, nebulae to nitrogen,
feathers to felines, solar systems to synapses.

She took a deep breath and used what she had.

WHILE YOU are limitless, I have limits all around me.
While You are unfathomable, I grasp at what I can know.
While You orchestrate the universe, I do my little part.
Thank You for caring, for hearing my prayers, and for being with me as I work.

She took a deep breath and paused to refocus.

If I don't pause here, right in the middle of my workday, right in the middle of so many words,
I start to rely on myself: *my* energy, *my* skills, *my* thinking, *my* processes, *my* direction.
We both know how that can end up.
Help me refocus on You, right here, right now.

> She took a deep breath and evaluated her pace.

I'M ENERGIZED to a point by the rush and the deadlines, but I learned that over time living at warp speed warps me.
Give me Your wisdom to know when to walk, when to run, and when to burst into sprints.

She took a deep breath and **reminded herself of the Truth.**

Your Word says in Christ I have all I need for life and godliness,
so keep pouring it in me now, Jesus.
I put on love and I rest because Your grace is sufficient for me,
right here, right now.

**She took
a deep breath
and
looked around,
and saw people.**

I USE MY FREEDOM to serve humbly and watch to love my neighbor.
I refresh myself with You, the Lover of my soul.
May I have Your eyes for the people in my path today.

EARLY AFTERNOON

She took a deep breath and felt His peace flow in.

Yᴏᴜ ᴀʀᴇ my Lord of Peace.
Help me keep perspective.
Help me remember You will fight for me, You will help me, I am not alone as I work.
Help me rest in that and not forget!

She took a deep breath and took care.

Details, Lord.
All the details of this day, all the doing,
I ask for Your help and guidance. People, projects, things, feelings, attitudes, conflict, failure.
Please refresh my mind that I may skillfully handle all of these details.

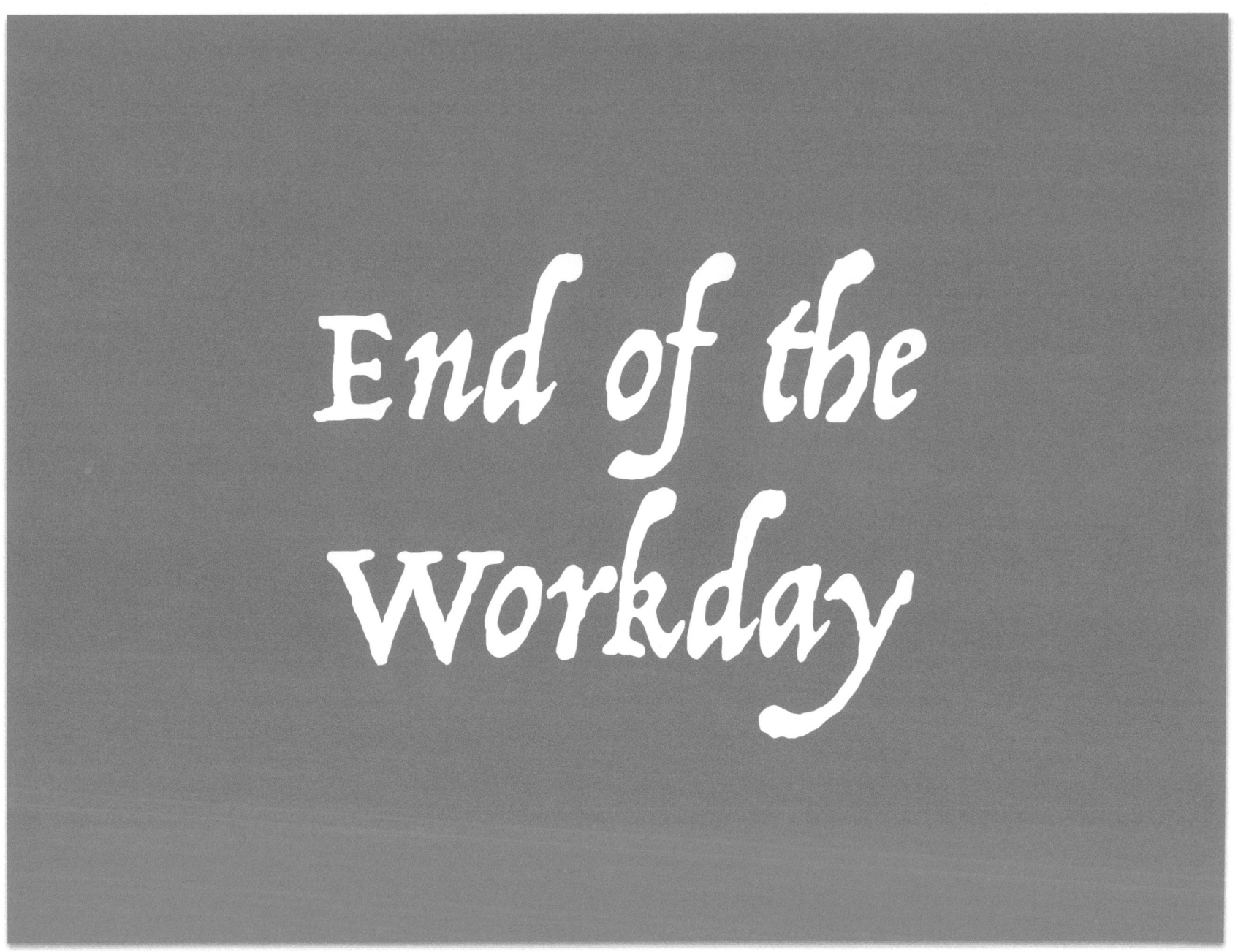

She took a deep breath and finished her tasks.

IN CHRIST I bring You glory by finishing the work You gave me to do with perseverance, purity, and love.
I run the race set out for me and fight the good fight of faith.

She took a deep breath and **recognized the change of the day.**

As the sun goes down, I become more reflective, examining the day and my soul. Help me reorient myself from being quickly efficient, task-centered, and work-minded to being thoughtful, to slowing my pace, to listening and loving more gently.

She took a deep breath and **switched from task manager to contemplative.**

JUST AS THE SUN moves toward the west to bring dusk,
so my mind moves toward You to bring closure to this day.
Sunset is my cue.
I pause and remember You.

She took a deep breath and embraced evening.

As the shadows lengthen, I offer You today's work and commit it into Your hands. As my workday ends, I'm ready to have deeper conversations with You whether I'm running the roads with little people or getting quiet during a commute.

Enough performance and agitation and travail; it's time to rein in my tempo.
It is time for me to remember that I am more than my job, more than my abilities,
more than what I produce for myself or my family or my company or my society.
Jesus, walk on the waters of my mind and say again, "Peace; be still."

END OF THE WORKDAY

She took a deep breath and gave God the credit.

I REMEMBER YOU as the One who gives me my abilities.
Just like the Israelites of old, I realize that You are the origin, the source, the giver of all good gifts.
You are always previous,
in abilities, gifts, circumstances, time, chosenness — it's all You, Lord.

Holy Spirit, be with me.
Let's review my day from Your point of view.
Give me eyes to see and ears to hear. Help the scales fall off my eyes.

She took a deep breath and looked for God's footprints in her day.

I KNOW YOU'VE BEEN with me today; You say You will never leave me, and I believe You.
So show me Your footprints, Father.
I long to delight in Your answers to my prayers, to recount Your kindnesses,
to amass experiences of Your grace.

THE EXAMEN

She took a deep breath and took stock of her day.

Help me think back on this day, Father:
beginnings, details, meetings, interactions with people,
the work I accomplished, the feelings I experienced,
my awareness of You.

Father, I see patterns within my own heart and behavior,
some good, some harmful, some so ingrained that I don't even think about them.
What do You have to say about my patterns: the rhythm of my day, my reactions to difficult people,
how I solve problems, when I feel overwhelmed, how I pray, what and whom I pursue?

She took a deep breath and looked underneath.

THERE IS ALWAYS SOMETHING underneath my actions, my reactions, my feelings, and my thoughts.
Help me get under there to discover more of me and more of You.
Help me comprehend the "why?" underneath why I do what I do,
and humbly turn to You as I understand myself better.

THE EXAMEN

Father, I invite You to change my thinking.
Help me trust You; You've been a good Father a long time.
Help me make You my first allegiance.

When was I close to You, and when did I miss You?

Was anyone or anything too important?

She took a deep breath and was transparent before Him.

What are You shaking up or settling down?
What are my distractions? What is choking out Your life within me?
What in me needs Your touch of life, needs Your breath of life?

She took a deep breath and reflected on heaven and earth.

Did my heart and life align with Yours?
Where did my mind settle during my mindless or repetitive tasks?
Who did I love well? Who did I not?

She took a deep breath and wondered why she was prickly.

What or who made me feel exhausted or irritable?

What was happening at a deeper level?

THE QUESTIONS

Did I live in Your steady peace? Why … why not?

She took a deep breath and **asked the questions.**

Was I where You wanted me to be?

Who were my trusted voices? Did I listen well?

THE QUESTIONS

What did today teach me about You?

THE QUESTIONS

> She took
> a deep breath,
> and
> thought about
> the life and death
> of the day.

In what circumstance did I have to "die"?

What life do I see from this death?

48
THE QUESTIONS

She took a deep breath and thought about the interactions of the day.

What would You have me learn by being with _____?
Should something different be happening in this relationship? Does anything need repair?
Why is there distance or delight?
Why am I drawn to _____? Why am I avoiding _____?

> She took a deep breath, and thought about how to reflect Your creativity.

How did You show Your affection to me today in a personal, loving, specific way?

How did I live creatively, thereby reflecting my Creator?

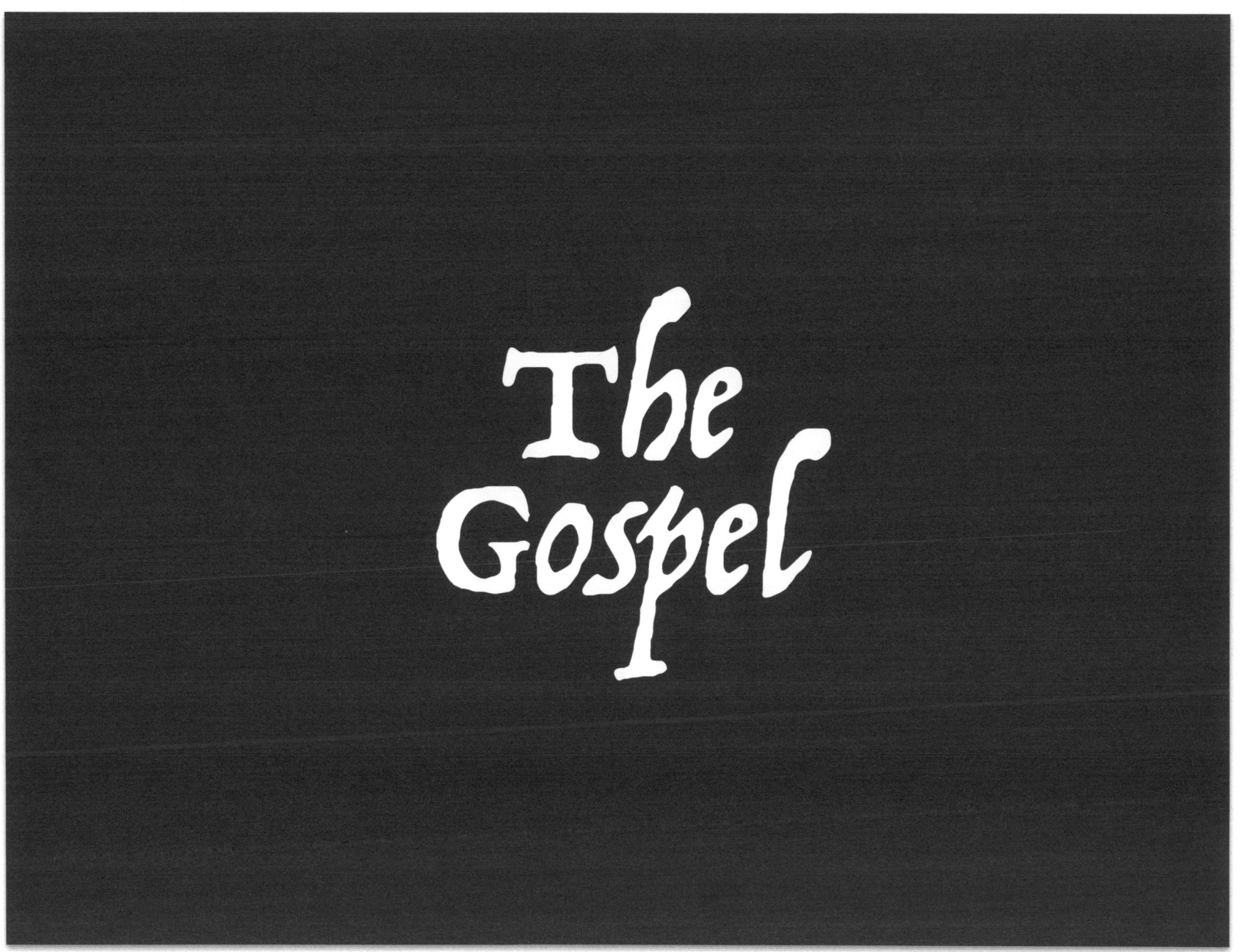

She took a deep breath and cried out for God's hand.

For the sake of Your Name, O LORD, forgive my iniquity, though it is great.
"Lord, save me!" Immediately, Jesus reached out His hand and caught Peter. "Why did you doubt?"
I acknowledged my sin to You and did not cover up my iniquity… and You forgave the guilt of my sin.
*Psalm 25:11; Matthew 14:30,31; Psalm 32:5

You see, at just the right time, while we were still powerless, Christ died for the ungodly.
God demonstrates His own love for us in this:
While we were still sinners, Christ died for us.
*Romans 5:6,8

THE GOSPEL

She took a deep breath and felt His gift of cleansing.

The blood of Jesus Christ His Son cleanses us from all sin.
I will forgive their iniquity and their sin and I will remember it no more.
Brought near by the blood of Christ. Your sins are forgiven you.
*1 John 1:7; Jeremiah 31:34; Ephesians 2:13,14; Mark 2:5

THE GOSPEL

She took
a deep breath
and
was
forgiven.

You have cast my sins behind Your back.
Who can forgive sins but God alone?
*Isaiah 38:17; Mark 2:7

THE GOSPEL

> She took
> a deep breath
> and
> His beauty
> was upon
> her.

All beautiful you are, My darling; there is no flaw in you.
In Christ, I am free.
*Song of Songs 4:7; Galatians 5:13

She took a deep breath and **praised her Savior!**

To Him who loves us and has freed us from our sins by his blood, and has made us to be a kingdom and priests to serve his God and Father – to Him be glory and power for ever and ever! Amen.
*Revelation 1:5,6

THE GOSPEL

> **She took a deep breath and flourished in His love.**

My soul finds rest in God alone; my salvation comes from Him.
But I am like an olive tree flourishing in the house of God;
I trust in God's unfailing love for ever and ever.
*Psalm 62:1; Psalm 52:8

She took a deep breath, received God's forgiveness, and soared.

If what You say is true — that if I confess my sins, You are faithful and just to forgive me —
then Hallelujah!
The weight and shame of disappointing You, of hurting others, of making myself upset —
it's off of me! I'm free again! Why would I ever choose to live any other way?

Blessed is the one whose transgressions are forgiven, whose sins are covered
… whose sin the LORD does not count against him.
*Psalm 32:1,2

She took a deep breath, sought out a quiet spot, and **enjoyed the Lord.**

It's the best part, isn't it?
Just being with You,
enjoying You
in the middle of everything.

THE PRAYERS

Glaciers carve a new landscape by pushing, reshaping, and transporting.
Their pace is slow, their rate is steady.
Holy Spirit, be a holy glacier, re-creating the landscape of my heart.

> **She took a deep breath and entered into the holy place of prayer.**

I like this time that is set apart (the very meaning of *holy*) for prayer.
I like to pull aside to be with You and talk with You, even though I can pray all day.
There is something special about our silent pauses. I want to listen to You.
Teach me how. Tune my ear to the spirit-to-Spirit conversations You want to have with me.

She took a deep breath and **moved toward quiet spaces.**

Jesus, You often withdrew to lonely places to pray;
You left the crowds. You stole away even when people were looking for You.
I'll follow Your example tonight.

THE PRAYERS

She took a deep breath and recalled the truth.

I consider Your instructions: Ask. Seek. Knock. Always pray; do not give up.
Go into your room, close the door, and pray to your Father, who is unseen. Don't babble on.
Are you asleep? Watch and pray so that you will not fall into temptation.
*Luke 11:9; Luke 18:1; Matthew 6:5-7; Mark 14:37,38

She took a deep breath and prayed into peace.

I lift my anxieties and stresses to You, remembering to "not be anxious about anything, but in every situation, by prayer and petition, with thanksgiving, present your requests to God. And the peace of God, which transcends all understanding, will guard your hearts and your minds in Christ Jesus."
*Philippians 4:6,7

She took a deep breath and prayed as He taught.

Our Father in heaven, we lift up Your Name as hallowed and precious. Your kingdom come, Your will be done, on earth as it is in heaven. Give us today our daily bread, and forgive us our sin as we forgive those who sin against us. Lead us not into temptation, but deliver us from the evil one, for Yours is the kingdom and the power and the glory forever. Amen.
*Matthew 6:9-13

She took a deep breath and prayed for those dear to her.

And this is my prayer: that your love may abound more and more in knowledge and depth of insight, so that you may be able to discern what is best and may be pure and blameless for the day of Christ, filled with the fruit of righteousness that comes through Jesus Christ—to the glory and praise of God.
*Philippians 1:9-11

Father, I am aware that for Christ-followers,
real living includes real dying.
Being a living sacrifice is worship.
Strengthen Your children. May we be faithful.

The Great Silence & Darkness

She took a deep breath and saw God's light in the stillness of the night.

I didn't realize how busy You are at night.
You spoke to Solomon, Daniel, Father Joseph, and Samuel in the stillness and peace of nighttime.
I lean into the darkness and choose to listen.

> She took
> a deep breath
> and
> knew
> You were awake.

He who watches over you will not slumber.
When I awake, I am still with You.
In the night, Lord, I remember Your Name. At midnight I rise to give You thanks.
My soul yearns for You in the night.
*Psalm 121:3; Psalm 139:18; Psalm 119:55; Psalm 119:62 Isaiah 26:9

She took a deep breath in the night and **saw with eyes of faith.**

In the deep of the night when my soul awakes, I will pray.
For those in peril, I pray Your protection. For those in confusion, I pray Your enlightenment.
For the spiritual warfare going on in the principalities and powers, I pray You and Your angels win!

> She took
> a deep breath
> and
> prayed for those
> still laboring.

For those caught in the toxic grind of trafficking, God, we pray for release.

For those who lack purpose, we pray for vision.

For those without access to work, we pray for meaningful jobs.

For those who labor productively and well, we thank You for their opportunities.

She took a deep breath and prayed for deliverance.

Part Your heavens, O LORD, and come down ...
reach down Your hand from on high; deliver and rescue me.
See, I have engraved you on the palms of My hands.
They will see His face.
*Psalm 144:5,7; Psalm 49:16; Revelation 22:4

THE GREAT SILENCE

Even in darkness light dawns for the upright, for those who are gracious and compassionate and righteous. Even the darkness will not be dark to you; the night will shine like the day, for darkness is as light to you.
*Psalm 112:4; Psalm 139:12

She took a deep breath and slept.

He grants to His beloved sleep.
If you lie down, you will not be afraid; when you lie down, your sleep will be sweet.
*Psalm 127:2; Proverbs 3:24

The Seven Sacred Pauses

Dawn

In Christ I am renewed. I embrace Your mercies for this day, and with creation I arise and delight in You.
I trust in Your grace to sustain me and Your truth to guide me. I walk by faith, not by sight.
I am filled with joy, knowing I am Yours and You are mine. I live as a child of light.
May Your face shine on me and may Your blessings fall on me, that the world may be covered in signs of Your love.

2 Corinthians 5:17; Galatians 6:15; Lamentations 3:22,23; Psalm 19:1-4; John 1:14b; 2 Corinthians 5:7; 2 Corinthians 12:9;
John 16:13; Song of Songs 2:16; Ephesians 5:8; Numbers 6:24-26; Matthew 5:44,45.

Mid-Morning

In Christ my work and the stuff of earth - vocation, relationship, and community - is sacred.
I work fearlessly and lovingly with all my heart for You, knowing I have a Master in Heaven.

1 Thessalonians 4:11,12; Colossians 3:17,23; Proverbs 31:13,17; Ecclesiastes 5:18-20; Acts 2:42-47;
1 John 4:18,19; Nehemiah 6:6-9; Colossians 4:1

Noon or Early Afternoon

In Christ I have all I need for life and godliness.
I put on love and rest because Your grace is sufficient for me.
I use my freedom to serve humbly and watch to love my neighbor.
I refresh myself with You, the Lover of my soul.
You are my Lord of Peace.

2 Peter 1:3; Colossians 3:14; 1 John 4:7;
2 Corinthians 12:9-12; Galatians 5:13,14; Song of Songs 2:10,13; 2 Thessalonians 3:16

End of the WorkDay

In Christ I bring You glory by finishing the work You gave me to do with perseverance, purity, and love.
I run the race set out for me and fight the good fight of faith. I remember You as the One who gives me my abilities.

John 17:4; John 4:34; Ephesians 2:10; James 1:4; Ephesians 5:1-4;
Hebrews 12:1; 2 Timothy 4:7; Deuteronomy 8:17,18 & 6:12

The Seven Sacred Pauses, continued

Evening, the Examen

In Christ I boldly rest in Your forgiveness, affection, restoration, and instruction.
In Christ, I am free. I make the Scriptures my home and my soul ages like fine wine with the lessons of the day.
I have the wisdom and riches of God in Christ.

1 John 1:9; Psalm 32:1-5; Psalm 130; Psalm 103:1-18; Song of Songs 4:7; Revelation 1:5,6; Psalm 19:12,13;
Psalm 52:8; Jeremiah 17:8; Galatians 5:13; 2 Timothy 3:14-16; 1 Corinthians 1:24

Late Evening or Bedtime

In Christ I create space for prayer. I pray intentionally, intercede thankfully, and listen earnestly.
I release my anxieties into Your care. I fix my thoughts on Jesus and all that is lovely and true.

Matthew 14:22-33; Luke 5:16; Psalm 139:23,24; Psalm 20   Philippians 4:6,7; Hebrews 1:2; Hebrews 3:1; 1 Peter 5:7;
Hebrews 12:2; Philippians 4:8

In the Night

In Christ I hold hands with trust and surrender,* lean into the still, quiet darkness, and grow wise. I pray for those in grim, fearful, godless places in the world, asking You for Your heart to be with them, Your hand to rescue them, Your face to shine upon them, and Your hope to be in them, for You are the God who sees. I hold firmly to the faith I profess.

Psalm 63:6-8; Psalm 86:5,15; Psalm 22; Numbers 6:24,25; Psalm 144:5,7; John 10:28; Revelation 1:16; Romans 5:3-5; Hebrews 4:13; Genesis 16:13; Jeremiah 23:24; Hebrews 4:14 and10:23
*phrase worded by Macrina Wiederkehr

The Examen Process

Day Sketch: What did you do today? Sketch it out briefly; bullet points are fine.

Clarity and Review: Pray for clarity, then with the Holy Spirit, review your day. To help you hear the voice of the Holy Spirit, check the list of **questions**: ask one or two of the questions. Listen attentively. What is He saying to you?

Look for **thankfuls ("Consolations")**: For what are you thankful? When did you experience God's grace and goodness?

Confession: Confess any failures, realizations about yourself and God, new understandings. Where did you fail or fracture **("desolations")**? On the positive side of confession, what can you declare about your heavenly Father?

Longings, Lessons, Looking Forward, Resolutions: What do you hope for, what do you long for? What are you looking forward to? Are there key lessons you learned today that drew you closer to the Trinity? Do you have any resolutions for tomorrow? Record them and be at peace.

The Questions: Pick one or two daily during the Examen to help you listen.

Holy Spirit, will You reveal to me …
Did I treasure You today? What competed for my affection?
When was I present with You? When did I miss You? Another way to ask: When did I move toward You today, and when did I move away from You? Or this: When was I alive and free in You? When was I bound up and tight?
Did my heart and life align with Yours?
Did I live in Your steady peace? Why … why not?
Where did my mind settle during my mindless or repetitive tasks?
Whom did I love well? Whom did I not?
Was I where You wanted me to be?
Who were my trusted voices? Did I listen well?
Was anyone or anything too important?
What did today teach me about You?
What or who made me feel exhausted or irritable? What was happening at a deeper level?
In what circumstance did I have to "die to self"? What life do I see from this death?

The Questions, continued

What were my "spotlight moments" of grace & glory (Psalm 84:11), of break-through, and of humiliation?
Did I order my life in such a way that I did what You wanted me to do?
What did I do? How did that affect us?
Father, I invite You to change my thinking.
Father, I invite You into this place of _____
(unrest, celebration, not knowing, joy, sorrow, anger, waiting, etc.).

Father, what do You have to say to me about _____?
You made me aware of _____.
Where did I invest myself?
Did my time, energy, & resources reflect the treasure of my heart?
What is <u>really</u> going on here?
Should something more or different be happening in this relationship?
Does anything need repair? Why is there distance or delight?

Why am I drawn to _____? Why am I avoiding _____?
What are You shaking up or settling down?
What are my distractions?
What in me needs Your touch of life, needs Your breath of life?
What was I afraid to let go of today? What did I happily receive?
Where am I missing the point or missing Your heart?
"Child, turn from _____ to Me."

How did You come to me today?
What did devotion look like today? (See Jeremiah 30:21.)
To answer the deepest longings of my heart and God's, what do I need to put aside?
(*Thanks, author Jim Branch.* An example: the wise men. They put aside much to pursue Jesus.)
What would You have me learn by being with _____?
How did You show Your affection to me today in a personal, loving, specific way?
How did I live creatively, thereby reflecting my Creator?

Photo Index
Cover:
1. The Morning
2. Pawley's Island sunrise
3. Sunrise splashes in the Baja, México
4. *Daily Light* devotional with my responsive stickies
5. Lynchburg, Virginia near the river, early in the fog
6. Sun in the fog & pines, Cohutta Springs retreat center, northern Georgia
7. Mirror image morning feed, Cohutta Springs, Georgia
8. Water lily, East Tennessee
9. Mid-Morning: the Value of Work
10. Camouflaged frog atop a cantaloupe, home
11. Extraordinary, ordinary Cinque Terre, Italy, from the Tower
12. Shopping for fresh fruit in southern Italy
13. Freshly-dyed yarns in a workshop in Addis Ababa, Ethiopia
14. Sand beads showing the industry of a sand crab, Magdalene Bay, México
15. A view of the Hong Kong skyline from across the river
16. "The main thing" saying found underfoot on the streets of New York City
17. A fresh palette ready for painting!
18. Haitian entrepreneur with 2nd Story Goods
19. Early Afternoon
20. Boy in the Words at the Lincoln Memorial, Washington, DC
21. Storm drain cover, Lynchburg, Virginia
22. Mountain stream flowing by an abandoned three-story mill, backroads VA
23. Best friends, Suki, Ethiopia
24. A simply beautiful *masseria* in the Puglia region of Italy
25. The exquisitely fine sewing of Burano, Italy
26. End of the Workday
27. Happy Haitian creatives
28. Dramatic golden sunset on the Baja trip
29. Sailboats at rest
30. Lengthening shadows, our front door
31. 2-sided wake in a variety of blue hues
32. Friends on the dock, Norris Lake, Tennessee
33. The Examen
34. Reflection off a dock in Shell Point Village, Florida
35. Single footprints on the Dunes, Magdalene Bay, México
36. Flowering on the trail, Cohutta Springs, Georgia
37. Sand dunes at Magdalena Bay, México
38. Dolphins leading the ship, the California Baja
39. Forever love lock on a Lynchburg, Virginia, bridge
40. Questions
41. Reading without electricity, the Guesthouse, Suki, Ethiopia
42. Diaphanous hibiscus blossoms, Turtle Inn, Belize
43. Sword-like iris leaves, home
44. Ice crystals on a tomato cage in our garden on a frosty-cold morning
45. Murano, Italy, waterway
46. Wheat stalks in a duomo, Italy
47. LeConte Trail, Tennessee mountains
48. Shattered tree trunk in the sunlight, Cohutta Springs, Georgia
49. This territorial woodpecker puffed up to intimidate another arrival
50. Frills on a crimson flower
51. The Gospel
52. Otter Mama floating and protectively holding her baby on her belly
53. Alaska: the tide is out and the birds are in
54. Rainbow promises
55. A melting iceberg, Inland Passage, Alaska
56. A yellow beauty, bright and cheery
57. Orca (killer whale) breaching and frolicking in Chatham Strait, Alaska
58. One of the oldest olive trees alive beside a Roman bridge, France
59. A gull spreading her wings near the Statue of Liberty, New York
60. Water spilling out of a pipe, the beautiful backroads of Virginia
61. The Prayers
62. A happy bumblebee finds rest and wealth on a Mexican sunflower
63. A glacier on the side of the road in Iceland, calling to us for a climb!
64. Burning a circular, pressed cardboard roll in the bonfire
65. Fishing vessel on Chatham Strait, Alaska
66. DIB boat on the coast as we enjoyed a bonfire at sunset
67. Letting go and praising God on the rocky coastline of the Inian Islands
68. Gargantuan sea lion looking up to heaven, Alaska
69. My neighbor Nancy's prayer cards … her requests go on her prayer board
70. Worn pole on the groin, South Carolina coast
71. The Great Silence and Darkness
72. Full moon in Iceland, shot from the porch of our AirBnB
73. A midnight view from the porch, Woodbine Avenue, East Tennessee
74. Rainy night in the back seat of a van driving the southern half of Iceland
75. My husband's chain saw chain before resharpening
76. Chains on a display wall in Spokane
77. The solar eclipse from Whimsey Farm, Tennessee, 8/21/17
78. Snoozing tiger beauty, Knoxville Zoo exhibit. Purrrrrrr

www.ingramcontent.com/pod-product-compliance
Lightning Source LLC
Chambersburg PA
CBHW041150070526
44583CB00004B/134